UNLIMITED INCOME

How to Win the Game of Life

KIERAN EKELEDO

All Rights Reserved. All the quotations unless otherwise indicated are from independent primary and secondary research. Written permission must be secured from the publisher to use or reproduce any part of this book, except for brief quotations in critical reviews, articles, sermons or presentations.

KIERAN EKELEDO
Copyright © 2015 by Kieran Ekeledo
Printed in the United Kingdom
Published by Success GPS
www.unlimitedincomethebook.com

CONTENTS

Chapter 1 Go Out And Get It 4

Chapter 2 Athlete Success Cycle Explained:
           The Three Keys To Winning The Game Of Life 19

Chapter 3 Coaching. 29

Chapter 4 Entrepreneurship. 37

Chapter 5 Corporate 48

Chapter 6 Empowerment 55

Chapter 7 Education 66

Chapter 8 Environment 75

CHAPTER 1
GO OUT AND GET IT

When you go after something in life and you really want to pursue it, there is nothing that can stop you apart from a lack of imagination and goodwill. The first thing you must do is to decide what you want to go out and get.

I want you to think deeply within yourself and find out what you want to go out and get, or what's missing in your life.

In this chapter we're going to cover **five action steps you can take to get out of your comfort zone and improve your results.**

The first thing we need to look at is something very important. With this you'll have super confidence in everything that you do. It will allow you to overcome setbacks and give you the extra edge you need. However, without this, you are likely to fall at every hurdle life throws at you. I know, I have fallen a few times.

It is near impossible to gain any momentum in pursuit of your dreams without… SELF-BELIEF.

1. INCREASE YOUR SELF-BELIEF

Self-belief is a character trait that provides you with the courage to pursue your dreams and aspirations with confidence.

For example, do you remember when you were learning to ride a bike? When you were first learning you were probably using training wheels or stabilisers to keep you on track while you built up the self-belief. When you felt you were ready, you decided to take off the kiddie wheels and you wanted to step it up a gear.

Perhaps you fell a few times before you got the hang of it. If you stand a bike up and nobody's on it, it won't move because it's the self-belief and action that enable you to create motion.

Let me take you back to a simpler time when I was a boy. All the popular school kids were very gifted athletically. They were able to do cartwheels and somersaults like there's no tomorrow. It was like a gymnast's school.

I considered myself a cool cat so I figured that in order to stay relevant in the year above I would have to learn to do somersaults too. I didn't know how I was going to do it, but I had the self-belief that I could do it if I kept on trying as I had seen others do it before. I knew it would be possible for me.

My success began with self-belief in my abilities. In time, my skills improved after practice, practice and more practice. It took me about eight months of repeatedly honing my skills after school every day until I was also able to do some of the same tricks that the cool kids could do in the year above. I used to go home and watch Dragon Ball Z to motivate myself. I would repeatedly attempt to do flips, day after day until I was at a level where I could do them time after time.

Now, I would like you to evaluate where you are at the moment by doing a quick exercise. Turn your head clockwise to see how far you can look over your right shoulder. Try this now.

Next, I want you to close your eyes and attempt doing this exercise again. Before you begin, close your eyes and visualise the point that you got to previously. Think of the point you reached but now allow yourself to imagine looking past this point by at least 20%. What would it feel like to turn your head as far as the new point? Once you have spent 30 seconds visualizing your improvement I want you to open your eyes and attempt this exercise again.

Were you able to look past the initial point you thought was your maximum less than three minutes ago? Did you notice that you were able to improve on your previous performance once you had summoned more self-belief in your abilities?

Have you ever had a dream or goal that others did not think you would be able to achieve but you went for it anyway and you managed to achieve your goal? Your success was rooted in your self-belief of your abilities.

> *"Self-belief is the seed of achievement that must be watered with hard work."*

The second action you can take to get out of your comfort zone and improve your results will allow you to achieve things that you did not think possible for yourself. It will allow you to improve all areas of your life and you will also have a lot more focus and drive.

If you don't take this step, you'll feel lost, like a person going through life without any vision or direction.

2. GOAL SETTING

Goals are the challenges you set for yourself to keep moving forward. They are targets that are specific, motivational and time-bound.

When we are born, our parents are the first people to set goals for us. Start crawling, start walking, saying our first word. These are targets set for us to achieve before we are 18 months old that will prove invaluable to us in the decades to come. When we start school we set academic goals like counting from 1 to 10, learning the alphabet and spelling our names. Our teachers set these goals for us.

At home you may have been given goals like washing the dishes, cleaning your room and packing the shopping away, etc. Your parents tell you what they want you to do, when they want you to do it by, and what you will need in order to achieve it. These goals were not the most fun but they taught you the discipline that you needed to get things done in a timely fashion.

As you get older, you get to set your own goals. When you turned 18, it might have been one of your goals to go out and have an amazing time with friends and family. Maybe it was to get drunk or find a partner to spend some quality time with. Whatever the weather, these goals were set by you before you were able to achieve them.

This reminds me of a story that Jeff Walker shared in his book called, "Launch". I would recommend this book to anybody who is interested in starting an online business. Jeff shared the story of a man who wanted to make his life one full of purpose. He wrote down in a journal over 100 things that he wanted to achieve before the days in this world ended. He began living on purpose and worked towards achieving his lifelong goals. Within 15 years of investing the time and effort into creating his list of goals, he had already ticked off more than two-thirds of the things on his list. This included getting several black belts in different martial arts, climbing Mount Kilimanjaro, getting married, having kids, becoming a millionaire and starting a charity. He set himself all sorts of personal, career and contribution goals that he achieved.

Three years ago, whilst going through a tough time in my life, I discovered one of the most inspiring people alive, Anthony Robbins. He wrote a book called "Awaken the Giant Within" that continues to transform millions of lives across the world year after year. He encouraged me to create a list of goals. One of the goals I set myself was to write a book that would help young people thrive. Less than two years later, I met Gerry Robert, an incredible guy who helps entrepreneurs to write books around the world. I met him at an amazing event where he taught me the tools I would need to make my dream become a reality.

Activities

1. To get started, I want you to write three goals down. Set yourself a goal to achieve one week from now, one month from now and one year from now. Make sure you WRITE IT DOWN. Write down the date you want to complete it by and what you want to achieve.

These goals may be something you want to be, something you want to do or something that you want to have.

2. Next write down why you want to achieve these goals. Why do you want to achieve this goal? How will this goal affect you and those you love? Why is it important to you?

In order to ignite the flame, the passion and the energy needed to attain this goal, you need to know why you are doing this because WHYpower will always trump WILLpower. With willpower you can summon the energy to get yourself up and get the job done but when you have whypower you are motivated by something deep inside you. You know why you are doing what you are doing and this will make you relentless in your effort. You can give 100% each time. This is something I learnt from Stephen Doran, a serial entrepreneur and life coach who is doing amazing things in the UK and around the world.

3. I want you to write down all the different resources you have available to you. This includes stationery, websites, software, people and information that will help you in pursuit of each one of your goals. Please think outside the box on this one.

I also want you to set checkpoints. Checkpoints are things or activities that you must complete that will let you know that you are on track to achieving your goal. Make sure that you identify the people you need around you. Who are the people you need in your life to help you achieve these goals? And where can you find them if they are not in your life right now?

Once you have a clear understanding of this, it will make the journey a lot easier.

4. Finally, I want you to reward yourself for each one of these goals achieved. The reward really comes in completing your goal but I want you to give yourself an extra gift.

Please follow through on these four simple steps and let's see what you are able to get done in the next twelve months. If you set yourself to a higher standard, you will unlock your true potential. Send me an email with your goals and I will make you accountable for what you will say you will get done.

Have you ever set yourself a goal that you wanted to achieve but you gave up before you achieved it, and you just stopped? The reason you gave up is because you didn't have enough legs to support your goals. You did not have a strong enough reason why.

If you were on top of a 20 story high rise building and you were offered £20 to walk across a 10 metre tight rope joined two buildings together, would you do it? The answer is probably not. However, if there was a blazing fire on the roof you were on and your child was hanging onto the tight rope screaming for help, I guarantee that you would attempt to climb across to save your child and escape the fire. This is because you were now more motivated to take action to change the current situation.

If there are enough legs or reasons to support your goal, such as family or finances that would be in jeopardy if you were not to take action, these legs of support give you the whypower to keep moving towards your goals. Whypower increases the probability of reaching your goals set.

> *"The thought of a goal is good, sharing a goal is great but working towards a goal with a plan makes you unstoppable."*

Create a vision board. This will crystallise the goals you put in your goal plan. The main reason why people don't achieve their dreams is because they do not make a conscious effort of really trying to go after them.

The third action that we will discuss will fast track you on your journey. It will provide you with a blueprint for success in whatever endeavour you choose to follow. Without this, you will make life a lot harder. I am talking about strategy.

3. CREATE A STRATEGY

Strategy is an action plan that enhances your performance.

When you are playing a game of football, the team will create a strategy by putting players in different positions to maximize the effectiveness of the team as a whole. You have 11 players on the pitch and the goal is to get the football into the opponent's nets. If you went on the pitch without knowing what position you were playing in and just wanted to kick the ball into the opponents net, that would not be very effective.

The fact that there is a strategy is what makes teams great. There are strikers who are focused in scoring goals for your team, midfielders who seek to control the pace and flow of the game, defenders who act as protection from the opposition from scoring goals in your net and a goalkeeper who acts as a last line of defence to stop the other team from scoring any goals. Some players alternate positions and others are fixed in their duty. These are all strategies that teams must implement to bring out the best of each other. This makes your team stronger as a unit.

Strategy is such an important component for successful living, that if you fail to put in place, you will pay the consequences for your lack of proper preparation.

I found this out the hard way when I first started boxing. I was scheduled to have my first unlicensed, white collar boxing match and I was confident that nobody could beat me. I had the head movement and thought I was a beast. That was until I had to do what beasts do. I had heart but no training. I thought you could win a fight with spirit alone. I never took my training seriously and would only go to the gym when it suited me. I had a 'laissez faire' attitude towards the effort required to be a true boxer. As I neglected my roadwork, when faced against a stronger, heavier opponent (8 kg heavier), I struggled. My lack of strategy in the fight and commitment to training meant that I lost the fight on a close decision.

Poor preparation prepares for poor performance. Proper preparation prepares you for great performance.

In my next bout, I was as fit as a fiddle, training twice a day, six days a week. Even though I only had four days' notice for the fight, I was prepared as I was training hard regardless. My routine of running, stretching, shadowboxing, sparring and padwork enabled me to make the most of any situation.

Putting in 90 minutes a day for six days prepares you mentally for any situation. When I got into the ring, I was able to stop my opponent early in the second round as I had worked really hard towards it. This was because I had a better strategy. I got myself ready for the goal that I wanted to achieve.

When you retire from sports, there are three ways in which you can leave:

1. You may leave through an injury before you wanted your career to end
2. You are no longer able to compete at an elite level due to old age
3. You decide that you would like to leave professional sports and pursue another career

Most athletes will fit into groups one or two; there are only a few fortunate athletes that fit into group three.

Regardless of how you leave football/boxing/rugby/athletics, you must create a strategy of what you will do if the end comes in one year, three years or five years. A prepared athlete leaves no stone unturned. This principle can give you the best possible chance of facing life after sports.

What areas of your life could you get better results from if you had a better strategy? Are there areas of your training and nutrition that you think you can improve to increase your longevity in sports? Are there areas of your personal life that you would like to improve such as finances or relationships? If you start approaching life with a different strategy and perspective you will be able to get a different result.

Just because you fail, it does not make you a failure. Failing to plan however is planning to fail. You are where you are in your life so far because you believe in yourself and you work hard. Start looking more at the bigger picture. Start thinking about the future and all of the great things you can achieve with the time that you have. Let the rest of your life be the best of your life.

4. TAKE ACTION

This is the only way to give you a fighting chance to win the game of life. Knowledge and skill will not get you anywhere if you do not take action on achieving what you want.

When you take action you will begin to expect better things in your life and not just hope for them.

Walk in faith and not by sight. Take action on your ideas and goals, when you believe that you can achieve them, half the work is already done.

Bugattis and Ferraris are fast, powerful, luxury cars but if you do not put the car in gear and press on the accelerator, it will not go anywhere and fulfil its potential. We, as human beings, are exactly the same. We have great ideas but we don't put in the effort and hard work to make it a reality.

Believe that you can achieve it and then take action in faith. If you are familiar with the law of attraction you will realise that Attr-ACTION finishes with action.

Whilst at university I wanted to start a business. Due to the fact that I had a lot of other commitments such as my studies, my jobs and boxing, I found it difficult to take action on my ideas. I did not have the business skill set to build a business, I failed at my first attempt and this led me to a state of depression and anxiety.

The overwhelming nature of everything that I was trying to do led me to my failure, however this has contributed to my more recent successes and for this I am grateful. I wanted to start a tech business even though I did not have any IT experience or a solid business plan. My lack of strategy did not help but I learned from the experience and therefore I am grateful for the loss. I had lost the battle but the war was far from over.

I once read a story on BetterLifeCoachingBlog.com that I know you will love. It's about a tiger and a crippled fox.

A man was walking through a forest when he saw a crippled fox. "I wonder how it manages to feed itself", he thought?

At that moment, a tiger approached, carrying its prey in its mouth. The tiger ate its fill and left what remained for the fox.

"If God helps the fox, he will help me too," The man thought. He went back home, shut himself up in his house and waited for the Heavens to bring him food.

Nothing happened.

He lay there in bed waiting for God to provide for him as he had for the fox, but instead he just starved.

Just when he was becoming almost too weak to go out and work, an angel appeared.

"Why did you decide to imitate the crippled fox?" asked the angel. "God has given you gifts and abilities to contribute to the world and make a living, while looking after the crippled foxes of the world. Get out of bed, pick up your tools and follow the way of the tiger! GO OUT AND GET IT!"

I only have one question today. **Which one are you, the fox or the tiger?**

5. LEARN FROM FAILURE

Learning from failure is the final thing you need to do to ensure that you win the game of life. Whether you are looking to pursue a new career tomorrow or in ten years, it is important that you learn from failure in everything that you do. This will allow you to turn your biggest loss to your greatest asset and your most painful memory into your most educational experience. If you fail to learn from previous errors, you will never get ahead in life because you will not change your approach to the task at hand.

Learning from failure is seeing failure as feedback of your actions, in order for you to adjust your approach to the task at hand.

When you first sat behind the wheel of a car you did not know how to drive. If you were to have taken your driving test on that day, you would have failed for sure. However, this would not have been a reflection of you as a person, this would have just meant that you needed to practice more in order to get better.

Even on the day of your driving test, you are allowed to make a few mistakes because the instructor knows that no driver is perfect. Your faults act as feedback to you so that you know the areas of your driving that you need to improve upon.

The most famous failure in recent history is a man named Thomas Edison. He was fixated with using electricity to create light. Mr. Edison failed over 10,000 times but he did not count these failed attempts as losses. He said, "I did not fail at creating the light bulb, I have just learnt 9,999 ways of how *not* to make the light bulb." This man's self-belief, vision and continuous effort are major contributors to a lot of the luxuries we enjoy today all over the world. This was all because of his incessant ability to learn from previous failures.

Michael Jordan is considered as one of the greatest athletes of all time. However, what many people forget is that he failed to make his high school basketball team. It was this failure at a young age that propelled his competitiveness and work effort so that he went on to become a legend in the NBA.

Steve Jobs, the founder of Apple, was fired from the company he started only to be reinstated a few years later. Prior to this he had failed to complete his university degree and had failed to generate as much revenue as fellow college dropout Bill Gates. After these painful lessons dished out in this game we call life, Jobs was able to launch three of the most innovative products and services this world has ever seen, iPod, iTunes and the iPhone.

Successful athletes, entrepreneurs and artists are glorified in mainstream media for their accomplishments, but they have at least five times as many failures that we never get to hear about. It is the mistakes we make on the way to our goals that make the journey that much more interesting. Do not be afraid to fail on the way to achieving your goal. Use your failures as feedback for your actions. If you keep on trying, then another opportunity may arise for you.

What can you learn from the mistakes and failures that you have made this week/month/year? Create a meaning out of these experiences that can empower you for the future and look at what actions you can do in order to get a better result in the future.

> *"The lessons you learn from the failures of yesterday are the tools that equip you for the opportunities of tomorrow."*
> *– Kieran Ekeledo*

CHAPTER 2
THE ATHLETE SUCCESS CYCLE EXPLAINED

I grew up around sports. Fitness was my passion and the gym was my playground. My mother was a fitness instructor and personal trainer and my father was a big martial arts fan. After three years of Karate, and finding that it bored me, I started doing Judo because I knew I enjoyed martial arts and competition. Over the next few years I competed frequently, winning at several regional events.

When I turned 11, I moved to live in Senegal with my mum. Senegal is a beautiful French speaking country in West Africa. This was initially a scary experience as I was in a class where everybody spoke French and I did not even know how to say "Comment ça va?" at the time. This forced me to adapt quickly to my new environment as I began to learn French and the culture.

As the years went by I learnt the language and the ways of the country. Life was good and I didn't have a worry in the world. Then came December 13, 2004, I got a call that would change my life forever.

Aunt P: Hi, Kieran? It's Aunty Peggy
Me: Hi Aunty Peggy, how are you doing?
Aunt P: I'm well thanks, how are you?
Me: I'm good thanks. How can I help?
Aunt: Your Mum is feeling under the weather so you are coming back to London a little earlier than expected. Pack your bags, you

will be leaving in two days. And oh yeah, pack like you aren't going back to Senegal!

Me: I don't know what you mean because I live in Senegal now, but OK!

After that conversation I knew that something funny was up but I didn't know what. Why was she being so cagey and vague about what's happening?

Nevertheless, I followed orders. The Playstation 2 and Gameboy Advance were packed so I had all the essentials ready to go. I was greeted by my aunt and my sister when I arrived in London. We drove straight to Royal London hospital from the airport to visit my mum.

My aunt had undersold the gravity of my mum's condition. When she told me she was feeling under the weather, I figured she may have had the flu or a headache, but I was met with a scene from "The Elephant Man". My mum was deep in a coma in the intensive care unit. Her face was swollen and she had dozens of tubes connected to her body and up her nose. She was not even able to breathe on her own. She had suffered an aneurism when she came to visit my sister.

The moment I saw her, I had to leave the room immediately. The sight of her in so much pain brought me to tears. **Seeing your mother on her deathbed is something that no 13-year-old child should ever have to see!**

The doctor called the family together and told us that she would be lucky if she lived 48 hours. I did not know how this was possible. The last time I saw her less than two weeks ago, she would do over 15 fitness classes a week and run half marathons in the morning to get the day started. As you can imagine, our family was heartbroken but we had not lost faith.

The experts were wrong! God, her inner strength kept her alive. She was left paralysed on her left side but I always thank God for sparing her life.

When I moved back to the UK, I was living between my aunt and uncle's house in North London, and my Dad's place in South London. In order for me to maintain my French, I went to Lycee Francais Charles De Gaulle as nobody in my family could speak French. This was a very new experience to me. My aunt and uncle were moderately affluent as they were barristers and surgeons respectively. This exposed me to a new lifestyle and a new level of wealth altogether. My school was filled with kids born with a silver spoon, peppered with kids from more moderate backgrounds where their families had made huge sacrifices to get them in.

My previous experience of learning to adapt to my environment came into practice again and I quickly found myself amongst peers I felt comfortable with. The years went by and I headed off to university. I went to study International Business Economics (BSc) at Swansea University. This was an amazing time in my life.

Whilst at university, I was living the student 'rockstar' lifestyle. I was a promoter for the students' union and worked in several bars. VIP entry, free drinks and exclusive house parties were a regular thing and I quickly forgot why I was there. My passion for martial arts continued there as I started boxing and kickboxing too.

In the four years I was in Swansea I had gone through the ups and downs of life. In my final year I had come to be more involved in the boxing club. As well as competing locally and nationally in boxing competitions, I was the treasurer as well as the coach for the boxing club. Our team won a championship and the notorious Varsity grudge match between Swansea and Cardiff that year. This was one of the proudest moments in my life but all things were not bright.

Whilst training at Welsh middleweight champion Chris Ware's gym "Funkypump Fitness" I was exposed to several professional boxers. This exposed me to some of the challenges that professional athletes have to face. Some of the boxers were doing amazing things outside of boxing, starting businesses with several income streams. Others were struggling to make ends' meet because in the fight game you don't earn if you don't fight. Therefore an injury can leave your family without food on the table for a while.

Although most careers in sports are not ended as tragically as my mum's career, a lack of career planning is eminent among athletes. I founded Success GPS coming up to my graduation and I am quickly being recognised as a thought leader in the fields of personal empowerment and life after sports. Success GPS empowers professional athletes for life after sports by identifying their passion and creating a strategic plan to achieve their future goals and aspirations. I have interviewed footballers from the Premier League, boxers and former Olympians to help create the content of this book. The philosophies of success that I learnt from these athletes that they have used to succeed in their lives will be shared with you in the pages to come.

THE LAND OF BROKEN DREAMS

The route to becoming a professional athlete or elite sportsperson is filled with many trials and tribulations. It requires a high level of dedication, sacrifice and discipline that most people are not prepared to make. According to Julian Sonny from Elite Daily, "1 in 1,010 high school boys who play American Football in the U.S. will be drafted to the NFL. 1 in 5,355 high school boys who play football in the U.S. will be drafted to the MLS (1 in 10,316 for girls to be drafted to the NWSL)".

These statistics illustrate the tough odds that every athlete must face when attempting to become a professional in their chosen domain…but this is only the beginning of the struggle.

The UK National Careers Service indicates that most paid athletes have other full-time or part-time jobs to supplement their income. This is because it is only a select few who are rewarded with the high incomes that we see on TV or read about in magazines. If you fit under the group of athletes who currently have to supplement your income, that's ok, because by the end of the book you will discover how you can earn an income around the sport you love. If you are fortunate enough to be one of those athletes, that is great, but there will still be storms ahead. The 6 to 9 figure incomes that you are currently receiving have a very short expiration date regardless of how talented you are. Fans may currently be worshipping at your feet. But you are in your prime. Mother nature does not spare anybody from aging and there will come a time in the near future when your body will no longer be able to perform the way it could in your prime. This is why it is so crucial for you to begin to set goals and strategize for life after sports.

Athletes who earn the highest incomes in the sports arena are the ones who are the hardest hit with retirement. Those who have never tried anything else often face a loss of identity, depression, drug abuse and financial hardships. Athletes who have had to supplement their income with other work or businesses have already developed other skills and identities outside of being a competitive athlete. Also, those who operate at the highest echelon of sports become accustomed to an expensive lifestyle. When your income stops, if you have not made wise investments or managed your money well, you can be struck by high mortgages.

> *"If you do not plan wisely, your upkeep may become your downfall."*

According to *Sports Illustrated,* "78 percent of NFL players face bankruptcy or serious financial stress within just two years of leaving the game, and 60 percent of NBA players face the same dire results in five years." Despite Premiership players making in excess of £1 million a year, the BBC reports that 40% of professional footballers go bankrupt within five years of retirement. There is an epidemic in professional sports and I do not want you to be another statistic.

HOW TO USE THIS BOOK

This book can be broken into three parts:

1. Go Out And Get It
2. The Transition
3. The Athlete Success Cycle

The first chapter of this book sets the tone for the pace and practicality of the book. The "Go Out And Get It" system can be applied to any area of your life. This five-step system is proven and tested to enable anybody who is being held back by procrastination to take action and build momentum. When I was at university and I was going through a very dark place, suffering from depression and panic attacks, I had to take time out to regroup and build myself back up. I came across a book called, "Awaken the Giant Within" by Anthony Robbins and it completely changed my life. I learnt principles that helped me redefine what I wanted out of life and empowered me to go after my goals. I was able to return to university and complete my degree as well as undertake leadership positions in the university boxing squad. What I am sharing with you worked for me and I am sure it will work for you, too, if you choose to apply it in your life.

The second part of this book 'The Transition" is where you can examine the different career opportunities that are available to you now and after your sporting career. After extensive study and research I began interviewing several retired professional athletes including Premiership footballers, world boxing champions and former Olympians to find out what they were up to after sports. They were all successful in their own right after sports and they all fit into at least one of three broad categories: **coaching, corporate work or entrepreneurship.**

In this section, you will be able to explore some career options you have available to you. You may choose to work in these fields whilst you are still an active athlete and earn an income around the sport you love. Otherwise, I would strongly recommend that you begin to develop skills and understanding in at least one of these areas. Your future is as bright as you want to make it.

The third and final section of Unlimited Income covers a success cycle that you will be dying to share with your friends and family. The "Athlete Success Cycle" is a ground breaking but simple system. After analysing dozens of successful people in different fields, there were three recurring themes that contributed to their success: *empowerment, education and environment*. Apply the lessons that are shared in the Athlete Success Cycle to your life and go through the different action steps given.

The Athlete Success Cycle can help you if:
- you want to prepare for life after sports
- you want to become a better athlete
- you want to learn basic money management strategies
- you want to earn an extra income around the sport you love
- you want to start a new career
- you want to feel more fulfilled
- you want to be surrounded by people that allow you to thrive
- you want to be of more value to your family and your team

If you answered yes to at least one of these statements, I would recommend you go over the Athlete Success Cycle at least once every 3-6 months.

We are what we repeatedly do, therefore going over the cycle once is not enough. Just like anything we wish to master, we have to go over it again and again.

"The difference between the student and the master is that the master has failed more times than the student has tried." – Unknown

You will not get everything right the first time but I promise you that the only way to win the game of life is to keep trying no matter how hard it seems.

THE CYCLE THAT LED THOUSANDS OF ATHLETES TO SUCCESS

So let's take a quick look at the three keys in the Athlete Success Cycle:

> **1. Empowerment:** This is where you begin. Empowerment will enable you to align yourself mentally, spiritually, emotionally and physically to achieve what it is in life that you want to achieve. (And I understand that you might not know what it is you want to do yet - I'll get to that in Chapters 3-5). At this stage in the cycle you begin to develop the mental muscle and belief that your goals are yours to have, you just now

need to go out and get it. As a result, your health will improve as well as the clarity in your vision for the future.

2. Education: This is the heart and soul of the cycle, where you begin looking at money management and multiple streams of income. Education will increase your awareness of the opportunities around you and will allow you to capitalise on your current circumstances personally and professionally. You use this stage in the cycle to discover how to manage your current finances and how to generate new income streams. It starts with learning about assets and liabilities and moves on to how you can do more with what you already have available to you. You will become more resourceful and observant to everything around you.

3. Environment: This is the final stage of your transformation, where you will create an environment that will nurture you to be your best self. 'You are the average of the five people you spend the most time with'. In this section, you will find mentors and create a mastermind group that will bring you closer to achieving your goals. You will not only learn the value of having the right people around you, but also the benefits of networking and adding value to others.

CHAPTER 3
COACHING

WHY BECOME A COACH

In my opinion, coaching is one of the most honourable professions in the world. As a coach, it is your job to get the most out of your team and/or client. Your success is measured by the results that you can get from your team/client. Some coaches consider themselves to be a master in their domain, but the best coaches are students and teachers at the same time. You are learning how you can get the most out of your players whilst you are teaching them how they can be their best self. You are investing your time and effort into their growth and development. Your role must be to add value to other people's lives.

The role of a coach can be both challenging and rewarding at the same time. Sometimes you may pour your heart and soul into the development of your client but they do not put forward the same level of effort and dedication. This will be frustrating as you know that they are not living up to their true potential, but do not fret. This is not a reflection of your ability; this is a reflection of the hunger and desire of your player. Help them identify why it is essential for them to see results and improvement and you will discover a player who is willing to give 120%.

The greatest athletes do not always make the greatest coaches. Being a great player or athlete does not automatically make you a great coach. Although knowledge and experience in your field is important, your ability to inspire, motivate and educate others is just as important. Floyd Mayweather Sr. and Freddie Roach were both notable boxers but they were rarely considered the best boxer of their era. Nevertheless, their careers as boxing coaches have been phenomenal. Each one of them has coached numerous world champions including Floyd Mayweather Jr., Manny Pacquiao, Oscar De La Hoya, Miguel Cotto, Peter Quillin and Amir Khan.

In order to become a certified coach there are qualifications that you will need to get. These qualifications are a method for the sports' governing bodies to set the minimum standard required to instruct others in that state or country. The length of these courses may vary from a couple of days to a couple weeks or years, depending on the level of specialisation that you reach. The cost of these courses may vary from £50 to several thousands of pounds. This can be financed in several different ways. The most common way to finance a coaching course is to pay for it yourself or to take out a loan. In some cases your sports club or organisation will fund the course. The Professional Footballer's Association have allocated funds for any footballer in the UK who has ever had a professional contract. There is also the option to do a government-funded course in the UK. If you qualify, the government will pay for you to do a course with very flexible options for repayment.

For example, if you want to become a Level 3 qualified personal trainer, the government will fund your course and you will be able to pay it back from as little as £7 a month once you start earning above £21,000 a year.

If this is of interest to you, get in contact with me on 07788291027 or email me at ke@unlimitedincomethebook.com and we can discuss what option is the best for you.

Here is a brief list (but not exclusive) of some of the coaching qualifications that you can get:

- Sports coaching e.g. boxing coach, football coach, rugby coach, swimming coach
- Personal training
- Strength and conditioning coach
- Fitness instructing

KEEP ADDING VALUE

Sports coaching and personal training are the most common forms of coaching that an athlete will pursue. Your first-hand knowledge and experience of what it takes to be a competitive athlete makes you a great asset to the sports industry.

The best time to begin your career as a coach or personal trainer is whilst you are still active. As a coach, you will develop an understanding of the game that you did not have before, therefore this will optimise your performance as an athlete as well. Many boxers, martial artists, footballers, rugby players, etc., open gyms and coach grassroots athletes whilst they are still active. It is not only a great way to earn an extra income around the sport you love; it also offers you the opportunity to give back to the community by helping others reach their full potential. The fact that you can coach part time is an added bonus as it can fit around the busiest of schedules.

In Figure 1 you get to see the differences and similarities between coaching and personal training to help you decide which one is best for you. This does not mean that you cannot choose to do both as many coaches are also personal trainers. I qualified as an assistant boxing coach in 2013 whilst representing the boxing team for the university and I am now studying to be a personal trainer. I am not telling you that it will be easy, but I promise you that it will be worth it.

EDUCATION IS THE KEY TO MORE OPTIONS IN LIFE!

Coaching	Personal Training
You are working with teams and individuals towards winning a competition or game.	You are working with individuals and small groups to help them reach personal health and fitness goals.
You will work in a sports club or gym (e.g. football club or boxing gym).	You will work in a gym, studio or outdoors.
You will be coaching at a time convenient for the team (e.g. mid-morning or early evening).	You will be training different clients at a time convenient to them: early in the morning, afternoon and at night.

You report to the club owner and shareholders. You may have personal coaching clients if it's an individual sport.	Personal training is like owning your own business. If you work in a club then you may report to the club manager but your income is uncapped.
As an elite sports coach, you will be working with the best athletes, preparing them for international competitions.	As an elite personal trainer, you will work with high net worth clients, own gyms and have video programs to duplicate your efforts.
The highest paid sports coach is Jose Mourinho who earns €18 million a year as coach for Chelsea Football Club according to the Standard. Life coaches can make a considerable amount more as Tony Robbins reports he has some clients who pay him $1 million a year.	The richest personal trainer in the world, Jake Steinfield, is estimated to have a net worth of $600 million. Although highly demanded trainers can make $300+ an hour, their main income is from authoring self-help books, motivational speaking, fitness programs and merchandise.

Another form of coaching that is not sport related but just as rewarding, is life coaching. A life coach helps people achieve their goals in life. People look at life coaches for advice in several different areas of their life. In the 21st century, there has been an explosion in the demand for life coaches in the West. With increasing pressures in work and family, people are turning to life coaches to support them on their journey. Rather than seeing a psychologist where you get the opportunity to open and share your problems, life coaching approaches things from a different perspective. Life coaching is more goal oriented whereby most of your focus goes on how you can be getting better results in your life. As an athlete, the trials and tribulations you face in competition can offer inspiration to other people who are overcoming the storms of life.

As a life coach you will be working with people from all walks of life. Athletes, entrepreneurs, CEOs, artists, musicians, stay-at-home mums and politicians have all sought expert advice from life coaches around the world.

Though there is no formal requirement to become a life coach, most life coaches are very driven individuals who have a passion for personal development and helping others. It is common for them to have studied Neuro Linguistic Programming (NLP) at some point in time to help them with their own mind-set conditioning. They have often overcome hardships like homelessness, depression, loss, bankruptcy or illness. These life experiences help them to relate to others and empathise with other people's struggles.

If you want to become a life coach it will be your story and your passion for life that will attract people to want to work with you. Hundreds of professional athletes have made the transition to become a life coach including Jovan Young.

BYRON BUBB

Ex-Grenadian international footballer Byron Bubb, now turned author and fitness expert, has found solace as a personal trainer. Byron started playing football in the park and then began playing on his local team, Kingsbury Park, when he was 11 years old and got picked up by Milwall as a youth. He went on to play for several teams including Hendon, Slough Town and AFC Wimbledon over the course of his career.

Like many elite athletes, Byron enjoyed the freedom that comes with football. "Having most of the day to yourself and being able to express yourself on the pitch" were some of the perks, however injuries and getting older are two things that no athlete can avoid.

In Byron's early to mid-twenties, due to a knee injury and football bureaucracy, Byron found himself without a professional contract. For the next few years, Byron wanted to make it back into professional football and did not really plan for life after sports. Nevertheless, Byron's grit and determination enabled him to land on his feet. Since retiring from professional sports Byron is a leading authority in the UK fitness industry and has built up multiple streams of income for himself. He is a personal trainer and assessor in London. He is also the assistant sales manager at Focus Fitness UK, one of the UK's leading personal training providers and the author of "10 Top Tips for Weight Loss Made Easy" which has received rave reviews on Amazon.

Life after sports was not an area that Byron had investigated in depth but he felt it made sense to stay in the fitness industry, as he was already a gym goer and cross fit enthusiast. The opportunity to educate and influence others to live a healthier lifestyle appealed to him so he ran with it.

Byron's Top Tip: Football is not all glitz and glamour; there is a lot of hard work and dedication involved. Do not rely on talent alone, as it can only get you so far.

Hard work beats talent when talent fails to work hard.

Instagram: @24HRFITNESSROCKSTAR

CHAPTER 4
ENTREPRENEURSHIP

WHY BECOME AN ENTREPRENEUR?

An entrepreneur is an individual who takes it upon himself to start a business, add value to the marketplace and make a profit. Entrepreneurship is an area that has the highest risk of failure but it also rewards those who are successful with the highest rate of return.

Entrepreneurs come in all different shapes and sizes. In the UK, most small business owners are aged between 45 and 54 (31%). Nevertheless, the world of business is not bias to age. About 36% of small business owners and co-owners are under the age of 45. This proves that you can start a business at any age and still make it work.

Education is the key to a successful business but formal education is not necessarily the answer. Although most entrepreneurs are educated up to a degree level or A level standard, there is a large percentage of entrepreneurs who do not have any formal education.

It can be argued that athletes make the best entrepreneurs as there are many similarities between sports and business.

- Athletes and entrepreneurs are both subject to competition in the league or marketplace.
- Athletes and entrepreneurs bounce back well from defeat. An athlete must come back stronger after a defeat.

- Entrepreneurs must test and risk failure in business to eventually have a successful company.
- Athletes and entrepreneurs need to know how to get the most out of their team.
- Athletes and entrepreneurs bring people together. Athletes do this through entertaining the public, entrepreneurs do this through employment opportunities and solving a need/problem.
- Athletes and entrepreneurs have a huge amount of self-confidence. The probability of surviving in either industry is slim, however, with the right attitude and work ethic anything is possible.

DIFFERENT TYPES OF BUSINESSES

Nowadays, the term "entrepreneur" is used to describe anybody who starts a business but there are different levels to business ownership.

As a business owner it is your duty to add value to the marketplace by solving a need, desire or problem. There are several ways that you can build a business but here are four of the most common methods for athletes.

Network Marketing Professional

Network marketing is a business opportunity that is very popular with people looking for part-time, flexible businesses. Network marketing enables you to build an international business under the umbrella of a parent company. Whilst you retail and recruit people into the business, the organisation will reward you on the productivity of your overall team.

Due to the low cost of entry (£35-£500) many people join the business in the hopes of getting rich quick but are disappointed when the results do not live up to their expectations. There is a very high attrition rate in this industry but do not let the statistics put you off from giving it a go. Network marketing offers a great opportunity to anyone, regardless of your social status or business background.

Infopreneur (Author/Speaker/Coach)

An infopreneur is somebody who can build a business through the sale of information, knowledge and expertise acquired over their lifetime. Infopreneurs are usually outgoing and have a message that they want to share with the world.

Infopreneurs will usually package their content in books, audio programs, speeches, seminars and online courses. This enables them to reach a larger audience and have more of an influence.

If you do not already have much clout in the industry that you are discussing, it will be beneficial to associate with people who are already known in your field. Becoming an infopreneur will be an uphill battle. Make sure that you have a strong will to get you through your difficult days. You must have a love for people to make it work.

This is the area where my passion lies. Empowering others to live a life that they love. I now give speeches and workshops across the UK at sports clubs, gyms and personal development seminars.

In 2016, I will be launching two new programs that have received great results in their pilot phases. The Athlete Mastermind Bootcamp is such a hit because of how it immerses my client's goals and desires into their subconscious to such a deep level over 12 weeks.

If you want to find out more about any of my programs and how you can create one of your own email me at ke@unlimitedincomethebook.com with the subject title ATHLETE MASTERMIND BOOTCAMP. I love what I do because I get to add value to people's lives every day. I would strongly recommend every athlete to seriously consider this as you have the ability to inspire millions of people around the world.

Start-up

A start-up founder is an entrepreneur who chooses to start from ground zero to build a new business. A start-up company is the business opportunity that has the most risk in entrepreneurship. This is because you are starting from scratch and you will be working in unchartered territory. There are support networks and mentors that are available to help turn your business idea into a revenue generating business. It is important to seek these advisors out in the beginning, otherwise it will cost you a lot of time and heartache in the long run. Gavin Heeroo's story is a great example of how to set up a successful start-up post professional sports.

Investor

An investor is someone who provides (or invests) money or resources for an enterprise, such as a corporation, with the expectation of financial or other gain.

As an investor, you need to already have access to capital. This is a great opportunity to make residual income. The most common things to invest in are bonds, businesses and property. There are different levels of risk involved in each investment opportunity so take due diligence before parting with your money. Robbie Fowler is a great example of an intelligent investor. Robbie has a range of investments including a successful property empire and several racehorses.

Entrepreneurship	
In sports	**Out of sports**
You have the opportunity to add value to athletes with a product or service.	You have the opportunity to add value to the marketplace with a product or service.
You are still involved in the sports/fitness industry so you can make the most of your contacts made during your career.	You are no longer involved in the sports/fitness industry so you must actively network to develop the key relationships necessary.
Your knowledge and experience puts you in a good position to spot the market's needs and challenges.	Your lack of knowledge and experience in this area requires you to seek validation from outside sources for the market's needs and challenges.
Basketball legend Michael Jordan is not only the GOAT but also one of the wealthiest retired athletes. With his Nike-owned Jordan brand and his stake in the Charlotte Hornets, MJ earned more than $100 million in 2014. His net worth is over $1 billion.	Former ice hockey and tennis player Ion Țiriac is a very accomplished businessman. The bulk of Ion's wealth came as a result of founding one of Romania's first private banks along with other business including insurance, retail, auto leasing, airlines etc. He is also a billionaire.
As your company grows, you may be required to hire staff to help manage and grow your business. In some cases, your company may go public and you will have to report to shareholders and a board of directors.	

ANNETTE LYNCH

Since the young age of ten years old, Annette had dreamt of taking part in the Olympics. She initially visualized herself reaching this goal in gymnastics but as time went on, Annette found another passion: volleyball. After many difficult years of moving up the ranks of indoor volleyball, Annette began to write her goals down under the instruction of her coach. This led to her being selected for the national volleyball squad and eventually becoming one of the pioneers of beach volleyball in Australia.

After Annette had won several state and national competitions at home it was announced that beach volleyball was to become an Olympic sport. This reawakened the opportunity for Annette to become an Olympian. In 2000, this dream was realised as she represented Australia at the Sydney Olympics in beach volleyball.

Although Annette had a Physiotherapy degree, this was not something that she was passionate about. Annette wanted to do sports media or sports marketing initially but found herself back in physiotherapy as she did not have the profile or the qualifications for her desired roles. Nevertheless, Annette's life changed in 2006 when she began to attend personal development seminars and found an identity outside of beach volleyball. Annette was now an entrepreneur and had begun to develop a vision for herself outside of sports.

Since retiring from beach volleyball, Annette has become a full time coach and trainer. She initially studied Neuro Linguistic Programming (NLP) and became an NLP trainer. This enabled her to uncover how our minds influence our results. She has written a fantastic book called "Success Beyond Sport" and has been coaching athletes from all over the world on how to transition into life after sports.

"I have eight steps in my book where I share with you how to retire from sports and keep winning. It comes from a mind-set point of view. How do you transform your mind and your attitudes so that you can focus on future success?"

Annette's personal battles of having to find a new identity after sports makes it easier for her to understand what her clients are going through and how she can best serve them in their transition.

Annette's Top Tip:

Think big picture. Step back and think beyond your sports career. Take a second to think of what you want your life to look like. Look at professional sports as a stepping-stone to something even greater. This will make the transition period that little bit easier.

http://www.successbeyondsport.com

CARL GREAVES

Carl Greaves is a former professional boxer. He first entered a boxing gym at the age of nine after watching Barry McGuigan win the world title in 1985. His local amateur gym only started accepting boys when they were eleven so he had to wait two more years until he could begin his amateur career. Carl continued boxing up until the age of 28, in which time he won the British Masters, Midlands area, WBF world title and challenging twice for the British title all at super featherweight. Carl loved the routine and discipline that boxing demands from its competitors but there was a certain level of politics involved that meant that some boxers were given more notice coming up to their fights.

Due to health reasons, Carl retired from boxing in 2005 after failing a medical examination. Although Carl felt like he had another year left in him, he was forced to hang up his gloves. Nevertheless, Carl has remained heavily involved in the sport as a manager, trainer and promoter. Carl always knew that he was going to get into the business side of boxing and the training side. Once word had got around that Carl was training fighters, he had a lot of boxers coming to him to seek his expertise. This led to him getting his manager's license followed by his promoter's license. With over 40 fighters across the country, Carl has become one of the biggest boxing promoters in the country. Carl Greaves Promotions has hosted more than 80 shows since 2007 without any major backers or TV contracts, which is a great feat in itself.

From a very young age, Carl began to build up multiple streams of income. During his professional boxing career, Carl was also an entrepreneur. He set up a furniture business when he was 20 years old, which he later sold in his mid-twenties after competing for the British title. Carl also puts on after dinner speaking engagements, including events featuring Barry McGuigan, Roy Jones Jr., Joe Calzaghe, Ricky Hatton and Frank Bruno.

Carl's Top Tip:

Travel more and get out of your comfort zone. Believe in yourself and your own abilities.

http://carlgreavespromotions.co.uk

GAVIN HEEROO

Gavin Heeroo is a former professional footballer. He played as a midfielder for Crystal Palace as a youth and senior, as well as for other English teams such as Ebbsfleet United and Cambridge United. Gavin realised he had a talent for football from a young age. Initially when Gavin was selected for the school team and county team, he saw football as a passion. It was only in his mid- to late teens that he was made aware that this could be an actual profession, so he pursued the dream with all his might and secured a spot with Crystal Palace's youth team.

When faced with life after football in his mid-20s, Gavin noticed that the real world was very different in lifestyle to that when you're a professional athlete. In life after sports, the world doesn't care about how good a footballer you once were. "When you get to the real world, everybody is just getting on with their lives. So you're not as special as you once thought you were."

Gavin's competitive nature and his willingness to take on a new challenge served him well on the road ahead. He knew there was more to life than playing football and wanted to succeed in something new. Since 2010, Gavin has qualified as a personal trainer and launched two successful businesses in the health and wellness industry. His first venture was launching a personal training company called Focus Fitness UK. When given an opportunity to partner with fellow teammate, Dougie Freedman, Gavin was able to evolve his start-up to one of the largest training providers in the UK in less than five years.

Gavin's secret to success lies in his willingness to learn, his self-belief, his work ethic and the opportunity to surround himself with people who are playing at a higher level than him. When he was 25, he already had his mind on building residual income and living life by design. This included being able to go away on holiday whenever he wants, which was not the case whilst being a professional footballer. Alongside Focus Fitness UK, Gavin owns an international nutrition business that gives him the opportunity to travel around the world opening new markets.

Gavin's top tip:

We are all born as an entrepreneur at heart. When you have your own business, you cannot sack yourself. Be in control of your own destiny.

www.focusfitnessuk.com

CHAPTER 5
CORPORATE

The corporate world is a term that is used to describe the rules and ethics that are in place when working for a corporation. In a capitalist country, like the UK, a corporation has certain laws, ethics, etc. that apply to it. As an employee of a corporation, it is your duty to follow the rules set by the corporation.

When I refer to the corporate world, I am referring to all occupations where there is heavy governance and rules that must be abided by including doctors, lawyers, teachers, bankers, c-suite executives and accountants, etc.

The corporate world is not usually a first choice for athletes in terms of career prospects due to the rigorous screening process. The extensive rules and regulations act as a barrier to many who would consider a career in the corporate world.

A career in the corporate world may be fitting for somebody who has always dreamt of becoming a lawyer, doctor or teacher. In the majority of cases, people leave the corporate world to pursue their dream career. However there are still a lot of people who find refuge and comfort in working for a larger corporation or organization. One of the major benefits of working in the corporate world is the opportunity to influence the market on a macro level. If you are a coach or an entrepreneur you have an influence over your own life and how you want to conduct business. When you are working in the corporate world and you are in a senior management position, the decisions that you make will have an impact on a larger number of people. For example, the decisions that the President of FIFA makes have a larger impact on football worldwide than the decisions that a football club manager makes.

The table below looks at the differences between working in the corporate world in and out of sports.

Corporate	
In Sports	Out of Sports
You have the opportunity to improve the administration of sports.	There are dozens of corporate jobs to choose from.
Your sports background may compensate for a lack of formal education.	Your sports background will not compensate for a lack of formal education.
You may have to get formal sports and management qualifications to make you more suitable.	You may have to get formal management and administration qualifications to make you more suitable.
You may get perks with the job including VIP tickets to games and other events.	You are likely to get other benefits including healthcare plans, life insurance, etc.

Lord Sebastian Coe is a British politician and former track and field athlete. He won four Olympic medals, including the 1500 metres gold medal at the Olympic Games in 1980 and 1984. Lord Coe's degree in Economics and Social History from Loughborough University enabled him to pursue a career in politics and sports administration. After a successful career in athletics, Lord Coe was elected as Member of Parliament for Falmouth and Cambourne in 1992. He was also appointed the first chairman of FIFA's independent watchdog and the vice chairman of the International Association of Athletics Federation (IAAF). Despite Lord Coe being under 60, he has already received some of the highest awards possible including the Lifetime Achievement Award in 2012.

PAT LALLY

Pat is a former footballer who played as a midfielder for several clubs including Milwall and Swansea City. He began his professional career at Milwall in 1970. His longest spell was with Swansea City where he made 161 appearances between 1973 and 1978.

During my interview with Pat, he revealed how he was able to transition from being a professional footballer to the Director of Education for the Professional Footballers Association.

Pat's journey began when he was playing for county and district teams as a youngster and was recommended to Milwall football club. Once signed by the club, the opportunity to keep fit and showcase his natural talent in an arena in front of a crowd of people kept Pat motivated and passionate. The relationships built with teammates were also like having a family away from home. Despite the travelling being quite arduous and lengthy at times, the pros far outweighed the cons in Pat's eyes.

Pat began preparing for life after sports by the age of 23. He knew that this could not last forever and wanted to be well prepared for the future. The biggest challenge Pat faced was figuring out what career he wanted to choose after the game. Whilst still active, he utilized the funding and resources available from the PFA to undertake a number of qualifications around business management and leisure management to name a few. Fortunately, a few months after retirement, a position in the educational department of the PFA opened up which he applied for and subsequently got.

After retirement, Pat continued to invest in himself by completing other qualifications and a degree. "The support systems by the PFA enabled me to undertake courses without having to fund those myself, which then helped me to build a CV when applying for jobs. This made my CV look far better than a CV with no academic qualifications apart from GCSEs, or back in those days, the GCEs."

Players often do not think of the transition at an early enough stage and may get caught on the blind side. Pat believes that from the moment a player enters professional football to the moment a player leaves professional football, they should be preparing for the career transition, whether it be in 5, 10 or 15 years' time. "Players should be putting in building blocks of academic, if not vocational qualifications that will enable that transition to be far easier than it possibly could be."

Pat's Top Tip:

Undertake some work experience in an area you fancy moving into once you retire. Most sports clubs have chairmen, boards of directors, accountants, etc. If you have an idea of the route you wish to follow after your professional career, ask one of the bodies within your club if you can job shadow somebody in that position to get a bird's eye view of the role.

www.thepfa.com

SIMON BARKER

Simon Barker is a former footballer who played as a tough tackling midfielder for the Blackburn Rovers, Queens Park Rangers and Port Vale over a 17 year career between 1983-2000.

As a kid, Simon loved playing football with friends in the park and realised that he had a natural talent. When he was put against tougher competition, he noticed that he was able to hold his own against the older kids. Once he got into secondary school, all the best players in the area would go to train at professional football clubs including West Bromwich Albion, Everton and Manchester United. At the age of 16, Simon signed for Blackburn Rovers as an apprentice for two years and spent the first five years of his senior career at the club before transferring to Queens Park Rangers where he played for 10 years.

Unlike many professional athletes, Simon had a long career (retired at the age of 35) and had achieved everything that he wanted to achieve as a footballer. The camaraderie of football and being part of a team are some of the things that Simon enjoyed most during his 17 year career, however when he did retire through injury he was ready for something new.

Before retirement, Simon was already on the management committee of the Professional Footballers Association (The PFA) so he was very aware of preparing for life after football. Simon had already completed his Level 2 and UEFA B coaching badges as he was keen to secure a coach or manager's role . After applying for a few positions and not getting anywhere, Simon was offered a full time post at The PFA within six weeks of retiring.

Simon's professional development continued after he was appointed as a Senior Executive at The PFA. Simon undertook management courses as well as completing a degree in Business Management and a Masters in Business Administration. The investment that Simon made in himself equipped him with the tools necessary for football administration.

Simon's Top Tip:

If you do not know what you want to do when your sports career is over then my advice is to make sure you do something whilst your career is still going. If you do a course and you don't enjoy it, that's fine because it may help you find out what it is that you enjoy and maybe want to do thereafter. If you prepare for what you are going to do after retirement, the transition will be much easier to go from professional sport to what my mum used to call "a proper job".

www.thepfa.com

CHAPTER 6
EMPOWERMENT

Empowerment is having the ability to motivate yourself and take action towards the things you want out of life. There are 6 main points that you can follow that will empower you today and for the rest of your life.

KNOWLEDGE

With knowledge you will be more confident at what you do. Without it you will never fulfil your true potential.

Knowledge includes facts, information, and skills acquired through experience or education that will help you be a better you. This will encourage you to be better and will give you confidence in pursuing things that you do not know much about. Many people say that knowledge is power because it empowers you to overcome your doubts and fears. The idea of life without competing in the sport you love is difficult to bear, but this is a reality that every athlete must face. When you equip yourself with knowledge, you will be able to look at life after sports with more optimism as you are aware of the opportunities that await you in the future.

Knowledge is an infinite pool of wisdom. The more you learn, the more you earn if you take action and approach life with confidence. Knowledge can be learnt in different shapes and sizes. It can be read, listened to, watched or experienced. You can watch it as videos, films, documentaries and webinars. You can read it through books, blogs, articles and magazines.

Do you remember your first driving lesson? Like most people, you probably stalled the car a few times as you were not able to find the biting point in time. You sat next to your driving instructor in the hope that they would save the day, as you knew they had more knowledge and expertise in the field of driving. As time went by, your confidence behind the wheel grew and you were able to read the traffic signs, know what most of the lights in the car meant and how to do all of the basic driving manoeuvres. You passed your driving test and were now legally allowed to drive.

The driving skill you developed was only a product of the knowledge and coaching that you learnt from your instructor. Your increased knowledge of driving has therefore empowered you to drive behind the wheel all by yourself even though there was a time when you were unable to do a turn in the road.

Imagine you were told that you were no longer able to compete at the sport you love, what would you do? Most likely you would discover other things that you are passionate about. Maybe you would find other ways to earn a living doing what you love.

Why wait until retirement to discover other things that you are passionate about? You cannot be a professional athlete for the rest of your life, so it is in your best interest to develop other talents that you possess so that you can be the best you can be in life after sports.

> **Failing to prepare is preparing to fail.**
> **Knowledge is the first step to confidence,**
> **and with confidence comes empowerment.**

EXERCISE AND NUTRITION

When you take care of this part of your life, you will be able to live full of energy and vitality. If you don't take care of this area of your life, you will feel lethargic and you will not give yourself the best chance at living a long healthy life.

Exercise and nutrition are pivotal to your long-term success. Exercise enables you to function at your best, both physically and mentally. Having all the money in the world becomes insignificant if you do not have the body and mobility to enjoy it with. As an athlete, you must already recognize the importance of exercise. It is best to keep it as an important area of your life.

What you put into your body is of equal importance. Nutrition is the food necessary for health and growth. Your body is a temple and it should be treated that way as much as you can. Eating clean food and having a balanced diet will increase your energy levels, hence your productivity will rise.

Have you ever noticed that you can feel more awake after a workout than you felt when you began? This is because exercise increases your energy levels.

Have you ever noticed that when you eat clean, you feel a lot stronger and focused? This is because good nutrition and a balanced diet are what the body needs to work at its best.

On the other side of the scale, if you were to sleep for 12 hours straight, when you get out bed, would you feel full of energy or lethargic?

If you were to stuff yourself at an eat as much as you like buffet with all the food and drink you like, would this make you feel vibrant or would it slow you down?

If you don't take the effort to eat right and exercise, how can you expect to win the game of life?

> *We are what we eat and we become what we repeatedly do.*

VISUALISATION

Without visualisation there would be no advances in technology, culture or design. Visualisation allows for visionaries to be born, which in turn shapes the world that we live in.

Visualisation is when you have a vision of your future; picturing what you can do and making this image as vivid as possible. Have you ever seen somebody else do something that you wanted to do? Or achieve something that you wanted to achieve? You imagined what it would be like to be in that same situation. To lift the trophy at a championship or to score the winning goal in a game, and then you went ahead and did it. This is the power of visualization.

I remember when I was preparing for my first amateur fight. I only had three days but boxers don't get ready; they stay ready. I was already in good shape. I did not know who my opponent was in the days coming up to my fight but I just visualized my victory. I imagined myself in that ring, moving and dancing around my opponent, slipping his blows and catching him with beautiful counter shots as I had done so often in training. When all was said and done and all three rounds were over, I had the victory in a quicker time than I had expected, with a second round TKO win. I had already pictured having my hand raised as my friends applauded in a distance before it had already happened.

I want you to visualize the great things that the future has in store for you over the next few years. Look back at one of your goals from the "Go Out And Get It" chapter and bring that goal to life. Visualise it in high definition. What does it look like? Who will be there? What are the features around? What will this goal smell like? What will you be able to hear and touch? The more vivid and clear this goal is, the more powerful this activity can become.

Have you ever had a moment of Déjà vu? This is often caused by the visualisation of a moment that hasn't yet taken place.

Your vision of greatness is yours to step into.

AFFIRMATIONS

The power of affirmations can often be neglected in everyday life. Affirmations have the power to shape your mind into positive thinking. The wrong affirmations also have the power to tear your life apart through negative thinking.

Affirmations are the words that we use and that we repeatedly tell ourselves. For example, if you were to tell yourself "I am a great athlete and I will go on to achieve more great things in life after sports," then this is an affirmation that empowers you to be the best version of yourself. Affirmations are the power of words that we tell ourselves.

Muhammad Ali was one of the greatest athletes to step into the ring. He was also one of the most influential orators in the game of sports. He often affirmed the exact round he would defeat his opponent in before the fight was ever fought. This would build his confidence and empower him to stay true to his word. One of his most renowned affirmations was, "I am the GREATEST".

Most people, when hearing those words think of Ali because he is now identified as "The GREATEST". The truth is that he had to affirm that belief before anybody else was to believe it.

Have you ever woken up in the morning, got off to a bad start to the day and from that moment, continued to tell yourself that this is going to be a bad day?

"Nothing seems to be going my way" or "I woke up on the bad side of the bed." Those are affirmations that add no value to your day or to your thinking. We've all had bad days but by reaffirming this, it will only bring more misfortune into your life.

Write down three things that you want to be, do or have.

This will become your first set of affirmations that you will tell yourself in the morning and at night.

Some of the affirmations that I use are:

- I will write a best-selling book
- I have a Millionaire Mind
- I am a kind, strong and loving person who works hard and plays hard

- I will build a positive environment where young adults thrive

Create a list for yourself and keep it with you in your wallet or handbag.

Look at it from time to time during the day and you will be amazed by the shift in mind-set and emotion that you will be able to create from it.

This brings confidence into your abilities and brings faith into your life. This is where all great things stem from.

We are good at giving affirmations to friends and family to build them up, but our own self-talk can be damaging and detrimental to ourselves.

Affirm the positive things, people and projects you want to attract in your life today. Feel the words, don't just say them.

PHYSIOLOGY

If you do not understand the basics of your physiology, you will not be able to operate at your highest capacity. When you are in control of your physiology and understand its importance, this will empower you to take control of your state and emotions.

Your physiology is the way in which you express yourself to the world. This comprises of your body language and how you breathe.

In communication, 7% is expressed in the words you use, 38% is expressed in your tonality and 55% is body language. This being said, your body language also has an effect on how you feel, and therefore will influence how you sound.

If you were to meet an old friend and they came to the bar with a hunched back, hands in the pocket and a scowl on their face whilst taking short breaths, you would assume that there is something wrong. On the other hand, if that friend were to walk in with a massive grin on their face, with their head held high and breathing in the air like they can smell flowers, you would have thought that they just won the lottery. Before any words have been exchanged, you would have an idea of how they are feeling.

I want you to learn to sit and stand in a position of empowerment before you are ready to take action towards one of your goals or aspirations.

This stance should enable you to feel confident, alert and prepared to take action.

Pay close attention to how your hands are, the alignment of your spine, your breathing pattern and your facial expressions.

Once you have practiced this position of empowerment, you will now have this in your arsenal to help empower you when you may be feeling down.

When was the last time you saw a champion walk onto the field with their shoulders slumped and their tale in between their legs?

Take Away: Our body language and breathing play a massive role in how we feel.

> *Take control of these two things and half the battle has already been won.*

ROUTINE

Routine will help you master a few simple disciplines that will be the key to you winning the game of life. If you neglect a good routine, your error in judgment will cost you dearly.

Routine is the habit of doing certain activities repeatedly.

As a child, you are taught that it is important to brush your teeth for good hygiene. As an adult, brushing your teeth daily becomes a part of your routine. If you one day chose to neglect this habit, this would make people want to spend less time near you as your breath would stink. This is the same case for good routines in life. If you neglect good habits that support your growth and achievement, you will not be able to attract the people in your life that will bring you closer to your dreams.

Everything we have covered so far is not to be visited once in a blue moon. These activities and principles must be repeated on a regular basis in order to get lasting results. You must:

- Visualize where you want to be in the future
- Feed your mind with knowledge
- Adopt good nutrition and exercise

- Choose powerful affirmations to say
- Be in control of your physiology

These are all things that must become a part of your routine to win the game of life.

By doing so, you will empower yourself to be the best you can be every day.

Every great athlete has had to adopt good habits and a routine to become a professional and excel. You have had to do so too, to get to where you are TODAY.

Nobody was born with the God given talent to play the game they love. It was the routine of hard work and dedication, day in and day out, the routine of sacrificing nights out with friends to make sure you make the morning sessions. These disciplines have enabled you to have the successes you have enjoyed so far in life.

Why stop now?

The Williams sisters grew up around tennis. Their father encouraged them to train hard. They did not win their grand slams through luck. It was by having a harder training program and a stricter regime than anybody else that has allowed them to be the best in the world.

These same principles are what have allowed Venus Williams to continue to win at life as she has launched her successful interior design company.

What routines do you currently adopt? What routines would you like to add to your life? What habits are not helping you move in the direction you want to in your life?

What disciplines would you like to play a more important part in your life? What habits would you like to remove from your life?

Put these habits in 2 columns, + or -, and start attacking them one by one.

Add one new habit to your life every 21 days and remove one habit from your life every 21 days.

Within six months, you would have adopted eight new positive habits and would have removed eight things from your life that were not supporting you.

This simple discipline has the power to have a MASSIVE impact on your daily productivity.

If somebody were to spend a week with you, would your actions display all the good things you are working towards in life?

> *A good routine can lead you to all the glory you seek in life but a bad routine has the power to crush everything you hold dear to you.*

CHAPTER 7
EDUCATION

LANGUAGE

When you develop your skills in this area, you enhance your ability to communicate effectively. If you neglect this area, you will quickly reach a plateau in terms of earning potential and in terms of self-improvement.

Language is the ability to communicate complex ideas and instructions verbally or visually. There are several types of language that can be used including sign language, body language and national languages that can be either written or spoken. In the context of this book, I will be referring to language in terms of spoken or written language e.g. English, French, and Spanish.

Your command of a language will determine your ability to understand other people and to be understood by others.

Each sport has its own language. One word can have different meanings depending on the sport that it is referring to. If a footballer were to ask for a cross in a boxing ring, they could be in for a surprise when they get clipped in the jaw by a rear hand. A penalty can be given in several team sports but the way in which a penalty is awarded will vary immensely.

What areas would you like to develop more understanding in? Where would you like to gain more knowledge? Answer this wisely and you will unlock what areas need the most expansion in your vocabulary.

> *Your language is a way to communicate with the world and others. Don't neglect it; nurture it.*

MANAGE

Learning to manage is one of the key skills that you need in life to become a great leader. If you don't learn to effectively manage your time, your goals, your finances and other resources, you will create unnecessary problems for yourself.

Management is taking charge of the different areas of your life. Good management skills are also needed to overcome difficult circumstances or challenges. Time can be the most difficult to lose track of. You may be busy training for games and competitions ahead as well as taking care of the family and enjoying time with friends. This is great but you must also find time to manage your finances and invest in your future. When you have an accountant and agent who handle the business side of your life, it is easy to neglect these areas. However, it is vital that you have an understanding of where you are and where you are going. It is better to gain some accounting skills and not need them than to need some accounting skills and not have them.

Learn the difference between income and expenses, the difference between your net worth and your cash flow. Robert Kiyosaki invented a fun game called "The Cashflow Quadrant" where you can get financially educated whilst spending time with family and friends. Once you have got to grips with this game, work out how much time per week you can dedicate to developing the skills needed for your career after sports, and get cracking.

"The future is yours if you go out and get it"

Remember when you were learning to drive. You would have felt overwhelmed with all the things that you had to do: changing gears, checking all your mirrors, finding the biting point as well as looking out for other cars. You managed to do it all and after a while it became second nature.

This is exactly the same. Are you using your time and managing your activities as effectively as you want to?

I challenge you to write down a list of all the things you would like to get done on a monthly basis and allocate a time for you to get it done. Feel free to delegate some of the tasks on your list but make sure that you have an overview of everything that's going on.

Whilst at university, I suffered too. I was starting up a business and I was overwhelmed by the amount of things that needed to be done. I had to manage people, resources and ideas but I had not yet developed the character and skills necessary to effectively manage a tech start-up. This business subsequently failed but I did not lose the lesson from it.

Many great athletes have reached the peak of the sporting world only to find themselves bankrupt years later. Mike Tyson had career earnings of over $500 million yet he was able to find himself bankrupt due to poor money management. Fortunately, due to his fame and hard work ethic, he was able to pick himself back up and re-establish himself.

According to a 2009 *Sports Illustrated* article, "78% of National Football League (NFL) players are either bankrupt or commit suicide within two years of retirement and an estimated 60% of National Basketball Association players go bankrupt within five years after leaving their sport."

Another article published on MindTheMoney.co.uk states that although premier league footballers earn on average in the region of £2.3 million a year, or £43,717 a week, 40% of retired footballers declared bankruptcy within five years of retiring.

These are not just facts and figures; this is the reality that is awaiting most top fleet professional athletes if they do not break the cycle.

Relate: Will you educate yourself so that you do not become the next statistic?

> *Manage your time well so you can take charge of your goals, your finances and the relationships in your life.*

DIVERSIFY

Diversification is a must for every athlete wanting to succeed in life after sport. If you diversify early in your career, this gives you the opportunity to reap the rewards ten-fold in life after sport. If you want until you are forced to diversify, you will be a victim of circumstance.

Diversifying in this sense is to generate other revenue streams outside of playing sports professionally. This may be from any of the career options already discussed including coaching, entrepreneurship or a corporate job as well as any others that you may think of e.g. acting/singing/dancing, etc.

Professional and elite athletes who need to take up second jobs whilst still active are already practicing the law of diversification. This will make the transition simpler; however, this should not prevent you from having a more lucrative life after sports.

When Ugo Ehiogu was coming near the end of his career, he had already chosen to do a coaching qualification that would serve him later on in life. He had also got himself involved with other investment ventures with friends as he continued to expand his portfolio. Carl Greaves had got his boxing coaching qualification before retiring. Once he retired, he continued his professional development as he got his promoter's license and manager's license.

This is a true form of diversification, as they could see that in the long haul they would have to find another means to live.

Floyd 'Money' Mayweather Jr. is one of the greatest examples of an athlete who is winning the game of life. In one of his post-fight interviews after beating Manny Pacquiao, he explains to the reporter the advantage of empowerment and education. Well before he got his nine figure cash pay-out, he had already visualized being the highest earning athlete in the world. He had affirmed that he wanted to make nine figures in one night and had stuck with a routine of positive habits that enabled him to reach this goal. The highest paid athlete on the planet has already created multiple streams of income in and around the sport of boxing. His leading boxing promotions company Mayweather Promotions has broken multiple pay per view records over the year and his clothing line brand The Money Team has a turnover of more than $1 million a month (All Access). Both of these enterprises are multimillion dollar companies. He was able to do this by mastering the third stage of the Athlete Success Cycle that we will cover later.

This is proof that you can be the best athlete in the world and still find time to build a successful empire alongside.

Fellow great boxer Manny Pacquiao has taken a different route of diversification to Mayweather Jr. He is pursuing a career in politics in the Philippines where he is currently a Congressman - another great example of what one can achieve when they put their mind to continuous and never ending improvement.

I want you to write down at least two different revenue streams that you think you could build over the next three to five years. On my Athlete Success Boot Camp, I help you look with more depth into the revenue streams that would fit your lifestyle best and get working on them immediately. Go to www.mysuccessgps.com to find out more.

Have you begun working on your future career goals?

If you haven't done so already at this point in the book, I want you to revisit the chapters covering different career transitions and choose at least one that you will pursue in more detail.

Will you take control of diversifying your income streams or will you leave yourself to be a victim of fate, living life on the edge?

> *Diversification truly allows you to win the game of life, not just the sport in which you compete.*

OPTIMISE

When you optimise, you will be better at what you do. You will be able to earn more, learn more and feel better.

Teach: Optimisation is to improve and alter what you are currently doing to get better results. You can optimise your performance on the field to become a better athlete. In this case, we are focusing on how you can optimise your business or second income stream.

Have you ever played a team sport where there was a weak link within the squad but with some adjustments in your formation you were able to overcome that and capitalize on the other team's weaknesses? This is exactly the same in life and in business. You must find the areas where you need to improve, make adjustments and then capitalize on the needs, problems and desires of the marketplace by adding value.

Have you ever tried to carry a bunch of items that seemed hard to carry at first but once you had moved some things around, it became a lot easier to manage? It is important to improve your effectiveness by changing your approach.

When I competed in boxing I had good footwork and hand speed, however my cardio was not very good. This forced me to spend more time skipping and running. My improved endurance optimised my performance so that I could be the best that I could be.

The personal training provider that I endorse for professional athletes and aspiring sports professionals have found that they have a higher rate of interest near gyms and sports clubs. This may sound obvious, but this can only be confirmed as it has been tested. This information optimised the company's conversion rate and hence this improved its profitability.

In my online coaching program called The Athlete Success Cycle, I work closely with motivated individuals who want to optimise areas of their life and business.

If you want to find out more about this email me at: ke@unlimitedincomethebook.com

Look at the area in which you would like to diversify your wealth.

1. Write down three to five activities that you will do to optimise your results. This may not be relevant to you yet as you will have to work on diversifying your income. If you have already done so, then this exercise should be done straight away.

2. As you diversify, look at the six key activities that are vital to your optimal performance.
3. Identify what activity you feel most comfortable with and where you feel you need the most improvement. Invest 70% of what you are best at and 30% on what you need to work on.

Sometimes it may help to get a second opinion from a good friend or colleague. Their objective feedback can be the key to opening up a goldmine.

Are you happy staying where you are right now, or do you want to optimise to be the best that you can be?

Optimisation and testing is the key to dominating your industry.

CHAPTER 8
ENVIRONMENT

TEAMWORK

When you work towards your goals with a team, you are able to make light work of any obstacle. Without a team to support you, the road to success can be very lonely and tiresome.

In this context, your team is made up of the people who will help you reach your goals and aspirations the fastest. This may be by collaborating with you on certain projects or it could be by offering moral support. Friends and family could make up a part of your team, as well as colleagues or staff that you have working with you on your objectives. Let's say you wanted to become an entrepreneur.

Your admin team, business partner, graphic designer, accountant, marketing executive and business coach would all make up part of your team.

No man is an island and this could not be truer than when retiring from professional sports. You will be venturing into a new world where you have relatively little experience compared to your peers. It is more crucial than ever to surround yourself with people who will help you grow and reach your full potential. You want to create a team of people who complement each other and are happy to work towards a common objective.

Whether you played a team sport or an individual sport, you always must be part of a team to reach your fullest potential. When you are in the pre-season period and you are training, the coaches, physiotherapists and everyone else who helps you to perform at your best are a part of the team. It doesn't matter how little or big their role is, it is important to make everybody feel appreciated.

On your pursuit for greatness, regardless of what you want to do in life, create a team of people who will hold you accountable to what you say you will do. This will push you to be more.

Have you ever felt like you're a part of something greater than yourself?

When you have the right team around you, they will hold you to a standard higher than you set for yourself.

APPEARANCE

When your appearance matches your purpose, people will take you more seriously. When your appearance does not match your purpose, this will put you at an automatic disadvantage to your competitors.

Your appearance determines the first impression that you give people. It is true that it is best not to judge a book by its cover, however when the cover is all you have to judge a book by, it will leave a first impression that may influence the way that you see the content inside.

When I refer to your appearance, this goes beyond the clothes that you wear. Your appearance also refers to how you are groomed and the tools of your trade. A footballer would never be caught without his/her boots, a boxer would not go to the gym without his gloves, a personal trainer would not go to work without his diary and a mechanic wouldn't go to a job without his toolbox.

If you were playing in the Champions League final, you would not go dressed in a three piece suit, therefore your appearance off the field is just as important. In sports, there are rules stating what is and isn't allowed in the game. In boxing, you have to have a gum shield in your mouth but in football you don't. In tennis you have to have a certain size racquet and in basketball there is a regulation in regards to the size of the ball you must play with. In life and in business, the rules are undefined, however they are just as important to understand if you want to be considered as a serious competitor.

If you are going for a job interview or a business meeting, it is important that you are well groomed and you are wearing a suit or a smart outfit. Although this is obvious, it is surprising the number of times someone's appearance is not congruent with the value that they offer.

When I wanted to change my identity at university from partygoer and promoter to athlete and entrepreneur, the first thing that I needed to do was to re-evaluate my appearance. I exchanged my homemade bar and designer clothes for my boxing gloves and blazer. It wasn't long until people began to think differently about me and take me more seriously. Whether we like it or not, people will define us by how we look and how we conduct ourselves.

Michael Jordan dresses differently now as a businessperson than how he used to dress when he was playing for Chicago Bulls. How does the way you dress and look show that you are taking your new career seriously? How will you choose to dress in the future when attending important events and meetings?

> *Let your appearance speak for you before you get a chance to open your mouth.*

EVENTS

If you attend events, you are opening the door to opportunity and self-discovery. A great event can be a life changing experience that can shape the way that you think, act and feel. If you don't attend events you are limiting your personal growth and development.

Events offer you the opportunity to collaborate and network with likeminded individuals.

I remember it like it was yesterday. Saturday, July 5th 2014, my good friend Cam invited me to an amazing event called Success in London featuring Les Brown and Chris Gardiner. He wasn't able to attend because he was on holiday but he had a free ticket for the event so he asked me if I could go. My initial reaction was to say "YES!! YES!!! AND YES!!!" but then I remembered that it was the same day as my sister's birthday. This left me in a difficult situation as she was heavily pregnant with her second child and I had not spent her last four birthdays with her as I was living in Wales for the past few years. Although I didn't know how, I told Cam to put me down for a ticket and I would find a way to go.

When I told Justina the news, I told her that I was prepared to miss the seminar of a lifetime to spend the day with her; she kindly refused my offer and insisted that I attend the seminar.

Success in London turned out to be a seminar that would change my life forever. There were many great speakers who were talking about how they were able to go from rags to riches in the space of a few years. At this event, it brought me back to the same euphoric feeling that I experienced the first time I read, "Awaken the Giant Within" by Anthony Robbins.

As the day went by, I had learnt so much and met some great people but it was the speech at the end of the day by Gerry Robert that really changed my life. He shared his story of how he grew up in the ghettoes of Canada to now be an international bestselling author who helps entrepreneurs and coaches to share their stories with the world via a book. Up until this point I always knew I wanted to write a book to educate the masses but I did not feel qualified to do so. His belief in me was all the fuel I needed to start me on the road to becoming an international author, speaker and coach. I signed up to his weekend course on the spot and the rest, as they say, is history.

If I did not attend Success in London then I would not have met Gerry Robert. If I did not meet Gerry Robert, it is unlikely that I would have had the confidence to launch my first book before reaching a quarter century.

Since attending this event I have brought my family along to several seminars and they have all found them highly rewarding and motivational. People who attend events, conferences and seminars are usually people who are hungry for success. This is a perfect place to find members for your team if you do not have a team yet.

Where are you going to meet the people who will change your life for the better?

> *You are one event away from discovering what you want to do with the rest of your life.*

MENTORS

Having a good mentor is the safest and most reliable route to success. With a good mentor, you will learn everything you need to know in your chosen domain. Without a mentor, you will not have a key component to winning the game of life.

A mentor is an experienced or trusted adviser. You can have mentors in different areas of your life that can support you in being the best you possible. All great leaders and athletes have had mentors or coaches throughout their career. This remains the same in life after sports if you wish to win the game of life.

The best form of a mentor is somebody who can guide you towards your goals whilst giving you an opportunity to ask questions when you need to, but this is not always possible. If you do not have direct access to the mentor you are looking for, you can always seek their wisdom through books, audio programs, videos and seminars, etc.

When I first heard Gerry Robert speak, I knew that I wanted him to mentor me as he had the results that I was looking for in my life. I knew what I wanted but I didn't have a concrete plan of how I would become an author, speaker and coach. Many years ago when I first picked up an Anthony Robbins' book, I had never heard of him but I now consider him a great mentor of mine. Although I have never met him, he has been able to coach me through some difficult times with his books, videos and audio programs.

A sports coach acts as a mentor to you as well. Your coach is able to push you beyond where you would be able to reach on your own. They will pick you up when you are down and will put you straight when you are side-tracked.

In the next 24 hours, identify two to three mentors who will be able to help you on your journey. If you have direct access to them that is even better but these people can be past or present. Many mentors have deposited their best ideas and life lessons into their material so you are still able to access some of their greatness through their books, videos and events.

Please find below a list of some of the places where you are able to learn from mentors if you do not have direct access to them yet:

- Seminars
- Conferences
- Exhibits
- Trade Shows
- Books
- Online courses

- Websites
- Blogs
- Articles

Relate: Michael Jordan has a mentor, Floyd Mayweather Jr. has a mentor, Bill Gates has a mentor, Warren Buffett has a mentor, David Beckham has a mentor. Do you have a mentor?

Success leaves clues so find a mentor whose footsteps you can follow.

ACKNOWLEDGEMENTS

I would not be the person I am today without the love, support and influence of many people.

Firstly, I would like to thank God for the opportunity to serve the people of this world. You have given me the strength to overcome some difficult obstacles in life.

To my Mum and most avid supporter, I can never thank you enough for the unconditional love you have given me. Regardless of what life has thrown at you, you've been able to face it with a smile whilst making others around you feel happy.

To my Dad, for all your support over the years. Although we did not have the regular father-son relationship all the time, I am happy that you have been a part of my life.

To Aunty Peggy and Graham, you took me into your house and treated me like one of your children. Even when I was unruly and not the best of kids, you still made time for me to make me feel like part of the family.

To Nanny and Justina, your words of wisdom although unwelcome at some points have proven invaluable over the years. Thank you for always believing in me.

To Michelle, thanks for being a great step-mum and welcoming me to the family on my arrival back from Senegal. It was a tough period in my life and your kindness made the transition that much easier.

To my siblings Teyha, Alyssa, Saira, Bryan, Faye, Sam and Sophie. Thanks for all the good times and laughs over the years.

Thank you to all my family who over the years have been there through thick and thin, especially Aunty Sylvia, Uncle Leon and Aunty Tammy. For those of you who came to support me in my first kickboxing competitions and came to some of my first motivational talks, thank you. I am really grateful.

To Andrew, Bubble and Bear. It is great to see you guys grow up into fine young citizens. Although we are on opposite sides of the world, I will always see you as my little brothers and sister.

To Tony Robbins and Gerry Robert, you awakened the Giant Within me and gave me the confidence to pursue my dreams. Without you two, this book would never have been written.

Thank you to all of my mentors Andy Harrington, Edward Smith, Dave Mutter, Napoleon Hill, Jim Rohn, Zig Ziglar, Les Brown, Eric Thomas, Stephen Cover, Robert Kiyosaki, Blair Singer, Gerry Robert, T. Harv Eker, Mac Attram, Brendon Burchard, Bob Proctor, Dale Carnegie, Mark Victor Hansen, Jack Canfield, Jeff Walker, Jeff Keller, Jay Abraham, Pat Flynn, Tosin Ogunnusi, John C. Maxwell Wayne Dyer. You all blazed the trail for me to follow.

Thank you to my boxing and kickboxing coaches and family who put me through my paces to make me better: Chris Ware, Avoen Perryman, Lance Caveman Jones, Daniel Ahern, Carl Mainwaring, Ricky Owen, Josh, Keri, Ryan, Wesley, Ray, CJ, Lloyd, Conor, Rob, Ryan, Michael, Alex, Kieran and many more. It was through witnessing the dedication and hardships that athletes need go through day-by-day that inspired me to write this book.

Thank you Opeyemi Omotayo, Tunji Ogunjumi, Stephanie Larson and Mary Thibodeau for helping out on the technical and editing side of the project. Your words of encouragement and support really helped.

Thank you to the Trillionaire Mastermind Team and Empower You Team: Josh Bardsley, Romain Neyses, Zohra Benjamin, Damian Slominski, Rhoda Nambassa, Sabi Hegysmi, Sunil Patel. Let's keep these mastermind calls going until we're enjoying the sunset on each other's yachts and islands as we change the world for the better.

Thank you to all my friends who have stuck by me through the storms and struggles of life: Courage, Kai, Tidiou, Evan, Camille, Pierre, Benji, Romain, Dom, Alex, Ray, Gabi, Fran, Nico and the Lycee British Section.

Thank you to all of the inspirational figures who have helped me get through tough times: Muhammad Ali, Floyd Mayweather Jr., Denzel Washington, Martin Luther King Jr., Eddie Murphy, Barack Obama, Bill Gates, Richard Branson, Will Smith, Michael Jordan, Ray Lewis, Roy Jones Jr, Prince Naseem, David Beckham, Oprah Winfrey, Gandhi, Bruce Lee, Jet Li, Jackie Chan, and Arnold Schwarzenegger.

I would like to say a final thank you to everybody who made the time for me to interview you for this book: Ketan Makwana, Tosin Ogunnusi, Stephen Doran, Ugo Ehiogu, Gavin Harry Heeroo, Byron

Bubbs, Annette Lynch, Pat Lally, Simon Barker, Carl Greaves, Ben Kilner, Tom Chamberlain, Simon Coulson and Mark Lloyd. Your stories and journeys make this book more practical for those facing difficult times ahead. I am very grateful for your vote of confidence.

Knowing your life's purpose has always been highly beneficial but now it is more important than ever.

If you know of any groups who would like to hire me as a **guest speaker** on any of the topics below, be sure to give them my email and number.

Self-belief
Goal-setting
Strategic planning
Taking action
Learning from failure
Empowering you
Investing in your education
Creating a nurturing environment

I also offer group coaching, one-to-one coaching and online courses that will help you on your journey to winning the game of life. J

I am on a mission to inspire, motivate, educate and empower 1 billion people over the next 20 years and would love for you to help me share my message.

If this book has added value to your life, please send me an email or text. I would love to hear from you.

*"Develop your skills, invest in yourself.
Nurture your talents and
enjoy the fruits of your labour."*

www.unlimitedincomethebook.com

Facebook: www.facebook.com/mysuccessgps

Instagram: @theathleteeducator

+447788291027

ke@unlimitedincomethebook.com

Stay Blessed!

www.ingramcontent.com/pod-product-compliance
Lightning Source LLC
Chambersburg PA
CBHW070548300426
44113CB00011B/1828